ESSENTIAL ELEMENTS®
POP SONGS
FOR ALTO CLARINET

ISBN 978-1-70515-019-1

World headquarters, contact:
Hal Leonard
7777 West Bluemound Road
Milwaukee, WI 53213
Email: info@halleonard.com

In Europe, contact:
Hal Leonard Europe Limited
1 Red Place
London, W1K 6PL
Email: info@halleonardeurope.com

In Australia, contact:
Hal Leonard Australia Pty. Ltd.
4 Lentara Court
Cheltenham, Victoria, 3192 Australia
Email: info@halleonard.com.au

THE MEDALLION CALLS
from PIRATES OF THE CARIBBEAN: THE CURSE OF THE BLACK PEARL

Music by KLAUS BADELT

GAME OF THRONES
Theme from the HBO Series GAME OF THRONES

By RAMIN DJAWADI

THE RAINBOW CONNECTION
from THE MUPPET MOVIE

Words and Music by
PAUL WILLIAMS and KENNETH L. ASCHER

Moderately, with a lilt

THE AVENGERS
from THE AVENGERS

Composed by ALAN SILVESTRI

Moderately, with intensity

HALLELUJAH

Words and Music by LEONARD COHEN

KERNKRAFT 400

By EMANUEL GUENTHER and FLORIAN SENFTER

HAPPY

Words and Music by PHARRELL WILLIAMS

Moderately Fast

SKYFALL
from the Motion Picture SKYFALL

Words and Music by
ADELE ADKINS and PAUL EPWORTH

Moderately Slow, Mysterious

HAVANA

**Words and Music by CAMILA CABELLO, LOUIS BELL, PHARRELL WILLIAMS,
ADAM FEENEY, ALI TAMPOSI, JEFFERY LAMAR WILLIAMS, BRIAN LEE,
ANDREW WOTMAN, BRITTANY HAZZARD and KAAN GUNESBERK**

Moderately, with a Latin Groove

HIGH HOPES

**Words and Music by BRENDON URIE, WILLIAM LOBBAN BEAN,
JONAS JEBERG, SAMUEL HOLLANDER, JACOB SINCLAIR,
JENNY OWEN YOUNGS, ILSEY JUBER, LAUREN PRITCHARD and TAYLA PARX**

Moderately

SEÑORITA

Words and Music by CAMILA CABELLO,
CHARLOTTE AITCHISON, JACK PATTERSON,
SHAWN MENDES, MAGNUS HOIBERG,
BENJAMIN LEVIN, ALI TAMPOSI
and ANDREW WOTMAN

Moderate Latin Groove

SEVEN NATION ARMY

Words and Music by JACK WHITE

Moderate Rock

HEAVEN

Words and Music by SHY CARTER,
LINDSAY RIMES and MATTHEW MCGINN

Slow Rock

DYNAMITE

Words and Music by
JESSICA AGOMBAR and DAVID STEWART

Moderately Fast

COUNTING STARS

Words and Music by RYAN TEDDER

SUCKER

Words and Music by NICK JONAS, JOSEPH JONAS,
MILES ALE, MUSTAFA AHMED, RYAN TEDDER, LOUIS BELL,
ADAM FEENEY, KEVIN JONAS and HOMER STEINWEISS

LET IT GO
from FROZEN

Music and Lyrics by
KRISTEN ANDERSON-LOPEZ and ROBERT LOPEZ

Half-Time Feel, Mysterious

WILDEST DREAMS

Words and Music by TAYLOR SWIFT,
MAX MARTIN and SHELLBACK

Moderately Fast

I GOTTA FEELING

Words and Music by WILL ADAMS,
ALLAN PINEDA, JAIME GOMEZ, STACY FERGUSON,
DAVID GUETTA and FREDERIC RIESTERER

Moderately Fast

VIDA LA VIDA

Words and Music by
GUY BERRYMAN, JON BUCKLAND
WILL CHAMPION and CHRIS MARTIN

With Intensity

THIS IS ME
from THE GREATEST SHOWMAN

Words and Music by
BENJ PASEK and JUSTIN PAUL

With Emotion

WE ARE THE CHAMPIONS

Words and Music by
FREDDIE MERCURY

Moderately Slow

BLINDING LIGHTS

Words and Music by ABEL TESFAYE,
MAX MARTIN, JASON QUENNEVILLE,
OSCAR HOLTER and AHMAD BALSHE

Fast, Driving Retro Pop

DON'T STOP BELIEVIN'

Words and Music by STEVE PERRY,
NEAL SCHON and JONATHAN CAIN

Moderate Rock

NO TIME TO DIE
from NO TIME TO DIE

Words and Music by BILLIE EILISH O'CONNELL
and FINNEAS O'CONNELL

LEAD THE WAY
from RAYA AND THE LAST DRAGON

Music and Lyrics by JHENE AIKO

YOU WILL BE FOUND
from DEAR EVAN HANSEN

Music and Lyrics by
BENJ PASEK and JUSTIN PAUL

Reverent

THE IMPERIAL MARCH (Darth Vader's Theme)
from STAR WARS: THE EMPIRE STRIKES BACK

Music by JOHN WILLIAMS

March

BELIEVER

Words and Music by DAN REYNOLDS, WAYNE SERMON, BEN MCKEE, DANIEL PLATZMAN, JUSTIN TRANTOR, MATTIAS LARSSON and ROBIN FREDRICKSSON

ANGRY BIRDS THEME

By ARI PULKKINEN